Be Happy

And

At Peace

Don E. Hickman

Published by: HappyAtPeace
http://www.HappyAtPeace.com
email: Don@HappyAtPeace.com

Dedicated to Nancy,

My beautiful wife,

My study partner,

My teacher,

My closest friend and companion,

Who has helped me to

Appreciate the

Gifts of Spirit.

Table of Contents

Foreword

To some people this title will seem whimsical and unrealistic. I suppose they may be right. Years ago, I had a similar opinion of Norman Vincent Peal's "Power of Positive Thinking." At the time I could not get past the words, "Think Positive." I could not reach into the "reality", the perspective, the attitude. It was many years before I began to appreciate the meaning behind the words; the attitude of being willing to be aware of positive aspects of what may appear to be a situation that can lead to only negative results.

Because of our limited experience of reality and our limited ability to process what we are capable of experiencing, we are able to comprehend only tiny bits of overall reality and typically focus the majority of our awareness on those aspects with the highest emotional value or intensity. Through the increased focus on these emotional aspects of the data we will subsequently fail to perceive or consider other aspects of the situation which go unnoticed. Unless we consciously, intentionally extend our focus beyond these habitual ways of perceiving life we will literally only see the world we automatically expect to see.

This is, of course, great oversimplification of the process of human perception and data processing, but I believe the model is useful, none the less. Few individuals consider the possibility that we actually have a choice in how we experience the world, a choice in how we 'feel' depending on the perspective from which we view life.

A choice to view life from a perspective of compassion and inclusivity fosters a sense of happiness and peace..

Be happy and at peace.

Don

Acknowledgements:

I wish to acknowledge Peter Vanderhoorn's wonderful picture that serves as the front cover of this work. It was taken some years ago looking up river from our place on the Mississinewa River. We could not have found a more appropriate cover picture.

Some of the photographs throughout the book were taken by my son, Ron Greystar of GreystarPictures.com. I claim him even if he uses a different professional name! He also was of great assistance in marketing and internet issues. Other pictures in the book include old family snapshots, snapshots around our place and pictures taken on one of our trips. The out-of focus quality in some of the photos is an intentional artifact, not poor technique on the part of the photographer or printer.

Pamela Schlechty patiently proofed the content and layout, provided computer layout assistance as well as general encouragement and support.

Cindi Benfield was very helpful with grammar/punctuation editing.

The members of the study group on The Way of Mastery that we attend provided the final proof reading. Thanks go to; Debbie Swisher, Anne Maddox, Marv Wiseman, Louise Personette and Kay Dougherty for this assistance.

I will only thank Nancy for the "short list", not all the things I could include. She has put up with me and encouraged me during the past more than thirty years, provided feedback, proofing and suggestions as needed. See the dedication for a longer list.

A PRAYER

Lord, we know so little
Of how to share Your love.
We strive for wealth and power,
And seem to always push and shove.
Human nature is what we call it,
But I just can't believe that
This is what You had in mind
When mankind was conceived.

I am sure that You saw farther
Than our short sighted plans.
I know You had to have more in mind
When You created man.
"In MY image" You said You made us,
But, Lord, how can that be?
Or is it that we just aren't quite where
You know that we can be?

If love is what You are, Lord,
And You made me like You,
Then there's still a lot of growing
Left for me to do.
I thank You for the blessin', Lord,
Of learnin' how to love.
Of learnin' how to share
Your special Godness from above.

1

Bartender Wisdom

Sun comes up in the mornin' time.
  Goes back down at night.
It doesn't know what's goin' on.
  It doesn't know my plight.
My woman, she don't love me no more.
  My boss told me to get lost.
My car broke down just yesterday
  And I just ain't got the cost.
This is the story I told the man
  Who stood behind the bar.
He just looked at me and said,
  "Brother, you know who you are."

I looked at him and shook my head.
  Now, what did he mean by that?
I got half mad and decided to go.
  I reached for my hat.
He said, "Now, buddy, don't get sore
  I'm not trying to be smart.
You've got to learn where your pain come from
  And you are the place that it starts."
He was slowly polishing glasses,
  Standing behind the bar.
He smiled at me, winked and said,
  "That's how you learn who you are."

He must have guessed how puzzled I was
    For he came around and sat down.
He poured for us both, smiled again and said,
    "Now, just you listen round.
You're a Child of God. You've got class, man!
    There's no need to feel burned.
Your problems in life are just friends in disguise.
    They're just here to help you to learn.
He sipped his drink and laughed out loud.
    He slapped his hand on the bar.
"Every thing that you find in life
    Simply helps you learn who you are!"

I don't completely understand what he meant.
    It's still hard for me to see
How the troubles that I find in life
    Are all here to help me.
But I do know that it makes a difference
    When I run head on into a wall,
If I just stop and look for lessons to learn
    I don't have to fight with it all.
I owe much to that friendly bartender,
    Who showed me that night at the bar,
That your response to what happens in life
    Is what shows you who you are.

Being Your Star

When you're feeling low
    And don't know where to go,
      It's not the world
        That keeps you tied up so.
You create the space
    And what limits there are.
      You're the only one
        That stops you from being your star.

Look inside your heart.
    Find the answers there.
      You'll find more truth there
      Than anywhere.
Following your heart
    Will take you far.
      Before you know it
      You'll be your own star.

All you have to do
    Is to trust your own light.
      It'll all come together
        When the time is right.
Let go of your ego.
    Release your power.
      Nothing can stop you
      When it's your hour.

The Being of Christmas

Christmas is the time of year

   To laugh, to sing and to spread good cheer.

For all the Christmas stories say,

   "the Christ was born a man that day."

He came from His World on high

   To give us a pattern for our lives.

The Christ Child came here to see

   If He could help us learn to be.

There are things the stories tell:

   Of angels and wise men wishing him well,

Of Mary and Joseph traveling afar,

   Of shepherds watching a beautiful star,

No room in the inn, no crib for a bed.

   And many other wondrous things were said.

But the most beautiful thing I can see

   Is that He came to help us learn how to be.

He wanted us to see in our lives here

    There's no need for depression, no need for fear.

He knew that we all could eventually find

    That blissful presence called peace of mind

That comes from awareness of His perfect love,

    The gift from our Father above.

This peace is ours when we learn to see

    How simple it is to just learn to be.

COUNTRY PRIDE

"It's a fine day," he said,
   As he laid down his hoe
   And walked over
      To sit in the shade.
He took a dipper of water
   And drank with a sigh,
      "That's got to be
         The best water God's made."
He was my grandpa.
   I was a kid.
      Lately I've begun
         To realize.
From him I learned
   A way of lookin' at life.
      I learned about
         Country pride.

"Go easy, walk softly,"
   Grandpa would say,
      "Not everyone
         Sings the same song.
Each one is diff'rent
   And has his own needs.
      No one is more right
         Or more wrong.
Every man's your brother,
   So watch how you treat him.
      We are all on
         The same ride
Loving yourself,
   Your world and your brother
      Is the meaning
         Of country pride."

When you look in the mirror
  And like what you see,
    And know you've got
      Nothin' to hide.
When the whole world's your home
  And everyone's your friend,
    And you know
      We're all on the same side.
When you see the beauty
  That's all around you
    And love everything
      That you find.
Then you'll know what I mean,
  What I'm a talkin' about,
    When I say
      Country pride.

When you feel in love
  With everything alive,
    Have a peace of mind
      That can't be denied,
When there's no one to fear
  And nothin' to hide,
    Everyone's your family
      And they're all on your side,
When life is a pleasure
  And a joyous ride.
    So full of wonder
      You lose track of time,
When you find heaven on earth
  And it's all right inside,
    Then you have
      Country pride.

DARKNESS OF LOVE

Darkness was everywhere,
  Nothing could I see.
There was no up or down.
  Nothing was there, not even me.
The Void engulfed my soul.
  There was nothing I could do.
There was no place to go.
  There was no way
    That I
      Could move.

My life was a mess,
  Nothing was right.
All of my dreams
  Had flown from my sight.
My hopes all run out,
  My heart faint with fright,
I followed my course
  On
    Into
      The night.

But something was different,
  Somehow I could tell.
From deep down inside
  Came the words "all is well."
My mind was at odds.
  Nothing could I say.
I just could not believe
  That
  Darkness
    Was the way.

  Then a voice said "Look!"
  But I didn't know where.
"Behind you, My Son!"
  And I turned to stare.
The beauty overwhelmed me.
  What a picture of love.
  What I had thought was darkness
    Was just
    A view
      From above.

DARKNESS

Darkness is only the absence of light,
   It leaves whenever light comes.
Darkness cannot exist in the light,
   It goes back to where it's from.

It's only here so that we can rest,
   Retreat and retire from the drum.
It disappears when we want the light.
   For, whenever we want light, it comes.

We can choose darkness, or we can choose light.
   It only affects how we see.
Sometimes we need darkness to rest from our work,
   For time to prepare the seed.

The choice is ours and ours alone,
   He will not force us to see.
His Light is there and He is willing to share,
   It is ours when we will it to be.

DANCING WITH THE WIND

A force, unseen, moves across the face of the deep.
Sensing but not seeing, we respond to the movement.
Aware of the subtle shifts, the rhythm and the pattern,
We flow through the intricate spirals and spins.
Breath for breath, pulse matched with our unseen partner,
With Joyful confidence and deepest Peace
We follow His lead.

In the Dance of Life the music we dance to, like our partner,
Is sensed, and not perceived by any physical means.
We follow His lead and the rhythm of the Inner Music
Through the constant touch of His Spirit.
We flow through life on the breath of the Spirit
In symphonic silence, like the gentle freshness
Of new fallen snow.

COME TO LOVE

Brother, won't you come along?
We're goin' where we belong.
A land full of joy
Where men and *little* boys
Are not afraid to
LOVE.

We're gonna make this land,
By just holding hands.
Love is all it takes.
Peace, we can make
A world based on
LOVE.

Come on Sisters sing our song!
Loving others can't be wrong!
Love is all we need.
Trees come from little seeds,
Miracles come from
LOVE.

Brother, it's me and you,
Doin' what we can do.
Let's all join hands
All over this land.
All this world needs is
LOVE!

EARTH ANTHEM

As I wander over this world of ours
   I am filled with Love.
The cool green fields caressed by deep blue ocean,
   Kissed by the warm sun from above.
The earth is a gift from the Universe,
   From God, our Father-Mother.
It's here we learn to love ourselves
   And our sisters and brothers.

The playful breeze strokes the young green grass
   And feels the beauty there.
The mountain tops blend with misty clouds
   And taste the love in the air.
The birds on high join with the wind.
   The whole world sees their love song.
All creatures below hear the touch of God
   And know that nothing can be wrong.

The Earth was freely given to man
   To be his loving home.
A place to learn to live and to Love,
   A fertile field in which to grow.
His brother beings on the Earth
   Are here to share this Love.
To teach us by how they live,
   And share the grace from above.

All men are brothers in this world.
  All creatures large and small,
Are here to form the universe
  Into what is best for all.
No separateness can be allowed
  On this our sacred ground,
Only Peace and Harmony
  And Love spread all around.

So let us all do our part
  To feed the world on Love,
And open our hearts to share the Peace
  And Light from above.
To give our Love will bring us Joy,
  And everlasting Peace,
And help the world to grow into
  The best that it can Be.

The Elf's Advice

I had wandered for days,
   Lost in a maze,
With a head full of doubt,
   I could find no way out.
I had spent my last dime.
   No friend could I find,
But what looked like the end
   Of the road was a bend.

As I sat and thought
   Of all the misery I'd bought
A new light came on.
   I was not alone.
High up on a shelf
   Sat this little old elf.
And without thinking twice
   He gave this advice.

What you think with your brain
   Is mostly insane.
What you know with your soul,
   Now, that's the way to go.
And I know there's a part
   Down deep in your heart
That can help you to see
   Just how you can be.

Now the conversation was light,
   The elf a delight.
I let my mind drift.
   I felt my mood lift.
You know, he was right.
   That was the source of my plight.
When the going gets rough
   I'm usually thinkin' too much.

As long as I go
   Only with what I know
There's nothin' I can't do.
   There's no way to be blue.
And I know in my heart
   Right where to start.
It's so easy to see,
   All we have to do is Be.

Evalyn's Wisdom

Lord, help me to see the little things in life,
  Those things we overlook each day
    And fail to keep in mind.
We get caught in the big things we see
  And miss all the important
    Ones that we could find.
Please help me to remember the little things
  That come along each day that
    Help us find life's rhythm and its rhyme.
Those little things that happen along our way
  Are really what makes the joy we feel
    That can fill up all of our time.

Lord, You are in the small parts of life,
  The sight of a friend, a baby's smile,
    The sound of music that we play.
In these things You guide us, Lord.
  And through them You
    Lighten up our way.
Help me realize Your wondrous
  Presence in these little things
    That I tend to ignore every day.
And help me to realize how much I
  Help or hinder all those I meet
    Through the little things I do and say.

Free Will

God created man in his image and gave him free will. He gave us each the freedom and the right to make mistakes, experience pain and even suffer, if we wish. No one can take this freedom and right from us.

He also gave us the freedom and right to increase our peace of mind and joy by reducing our suffering through learning not to resist the inevitability of mistakes; and pain. No one can take this freedom and right away from us.

He gave us the further freedom and right to move closer to Him and minimize our mistakes and the resulting pain by becoming increasingly aware of His Divine Laws of cause and effect, by relinquishing our need to direct the course of events and surrender to His Direction and Guidance through increasing our awareness and understanding of the Perfection of His Creation. No one can take this freedom and right from us.

He has expressed His Preference for us to pursue peace of mind and draw closer to Him in joy. He provided His Son and His Spirit to assist us in this process.

FORGIVENESS

Belief is simply
The language of the mind,
Symbolically representing reality
From a particular point of view.
Forgiveness is the awareness
That languages are neither
Good nor evil. They are simply
Tools for communication.
Judgment is the belief
That God made a mistake,
And that it is the duty of man
To show God the error of His ways.
Forgiveness is the acceptance
Of the Divine Order
Of the Universe that was placed
In motion by the Creator.
Fear is a sense of being
Fragile and defenseless,
At the mercy of a vicious,
Hostile universe.
Forgiveness is the recognition that
"All things work together for good.
There are no exceptions
Except in the ego's judgment."*

*A COURSE IN MIRIACLES Text, p. 59, Foundation for Inner Peace, Tiburon, Ca. 1975

23

GOD IS OUR FATHER

God is our Father.

    The Earth is our Mother.

    God's Sons all, are we.

We can live

    And love together

    In perfect harmony.

There is nothing

    Here to fear.

    Love is all around

If we'll just

    Open up our hearts

    And listen to the sound

Of God, our Father,

    And the Earth, our Mother,

    And God's Sons all around.

LIGHT and LOVE

    Will be our way,

    And PEACE OF MIND abound.

GIVE IT UP

The only way to keep it is to give it up.
  You can't have more joy than what fills your cup.
If you try to hang on to what you've got,
  You'll find your cup won't hold another drop.
In the process of growing we never lose.
  We only turn loose of what we choose.
Things that we need are always there,
    The things we let go of
      Are the things
        We can spare.

When I feel myself hanging on to things.
  When the bells in my life seldom ring.
I check out my pockets for things I don't need.
  I recycle my gifts, not give in to greed.
The things that life gives us are not just ours.
  They belong to all, just like the spring showers.
By trying to keep them and make them "mine",
    I just slow my growth
      And confuse
        My mind.

GOD'S LOVE IS CALLING US HOME

Whenever we fear,
　Feel full of despair,
　　When we feel
　　　So all alone.
　　　　God's Love is near.
　　　　　It overcomes all fear.
　　　　　It reaches us
　　　　　　Wherever we roam.
　　　　　God's Love
　　　　　　Is calling us home.

　Day replaces night.
　　Nothing hides from light.
　　Love will always
　　　Claim its own.
　　　　Our suffering is not real.
　　　　　It's only how we feel.
　　　　This world
　　　　　Is not our own.
　　　　　God's Love is
　　　　　　Calling us home.

　The choice is day or night,
　　Darkness or light,
　　　Togetherness
　　　Or being alone.
　　　　It's a choice we make each day,
　　　　　Each minute along the way,
　　　　It's a decision
　　　　　That each must own.
　　　　　But, God's Love is
　　　　　　Calling us home.

Gifts Given and Received

Life brings peace to me
   As I continue to see
That the way of life
   Need not lead to strife
   But can always peaceful be.

The way we choose to perceive,
   In what we choose to believe,
With the life that we live
   Are the gifts that we give
   As well as the ones we receive.

GOD'S WORD OF LOVE

The Love of God is the Word
That chases fear away.
It is the bright and shining Son
That starts a brand new day.

His Word, LOVE, ends all fear
And give us peace of mind.
God's Word cannot be overrun,
Nor can it be outshined.

God's Word has no equal.
No power can bring it down.
It only fails when we refuse
To ask it to come around.

His Word, LOVE, is always near.
It never disappears.
Whenever we choose it to be,
His Peace of Mind is here.

Whenever we see darkness
And feel a heavy weight,
His Word, LOVE, will lighten both,
And straighten out our way,

We simply have to choose
To focus on the light.
Darkness has no power at all
When LOVE is shining bright.

GOD'S SYMPHONY

I was walking on a moonlit night
Down by the old highway.
The stars and moon were oh so bright.
It was almost as light as day.
I heard a soft and singing sound
I could not identify.
It seemed to come from all around,
From the ground and from the sky.

I searched all around but I could not find
The source of that beautiful sound.
It followed where ever my trail would wind,
But its maker could not be found.
I finally gave up, my hunt I ceased,
And I listened to the whispering notes.
As I listened I felt an inner peace.
My soul seemed to actually float.

I felt myself blend with the ground and the trees.
I became part of the sky.
I knew how to soar and ride on the breeze.
I watched the whole scene float by.
The music was part of my every thought.
The world was a symphony.
The pleasure I knew could never be bought,
As I learned of God's gift to me.

He spoke in the sea. He spoke in the wind.
His message was so clear to me.
All creation was seen as perfect by Him.
It's just what He wants it to be.
Our problem is we just don't hear
The sweet song that continually plays.
We fail to listen for the melody dear,
That will guide us all of our days.

GOD'S HANDS HOLD IT ALL

Deep inside my soul
    This one thing I know.
The universe is whole,
    Because God made it so.

Nothin's ever wrong.
    Everything's where it belongs.
Perfection is the only song,
    As sure as day always comes along.

When I can't seem to understand,
    I know that it is still His plan.
His order of love will always stand.
    We just have to hold His hand.

Even when I cannot see,
    All I have to do is be.
I know His order includes me.
    Yielding to Him is just reality.

God's Hands hold it all.
    His way can never fall.
Nothing can ever build a wall
    Strong enough to block His call.

His Love is the only way,
    The only true light of day.
Our real wish is His Will to obey.
    His Praises are all we can ever say.

Holding On To The Pain

How do I learn to surrender?
  Can I ever learn to let go?
What do I do with the pieces
  Of my tantrum throwing ego?
My pretending control is illusion!
  I know life isn't really that way.
But I don't like to face the confusion
  When I can't make things go my way.

I can pretend to be very enlightened
  And act as if I knew all along,
That the world would never co-operate
  As I tried to right all its wrongs.
But the reality is very much different.
  Calm and rational is something I'm not!
If not for my non-violent convictions,
  Several people would probably be shot!

My ego is bruised and battered.
  I feel such rage and defeat!
But I know that it is just the energy
  I need to use to get out of my seat.
The world doesn't need me to change it,
  It's designed to work like it is.
My job is to flow with the current,
  Designing the river is His.

I believe God knows what He is doing.
  And I would never want to complain,
But I can't seem to always remember
  How to not hold on to the pain.
My suffering is not His creation;
  He did not design in the strain.
It's our job to follow His pattern
  And not to hold on to the pain

HE WAS DIF'RENT

Now gather 'round, brothers.
You sisters come, too.
I've a story to relate,
'Specially *for you.*
It's a strange tale you'll hear
'Bout a man long ago,
He was dif'rent from others
In many ways I've been told.

He never seemed to care
For the ways of this earth.
He did not need treasure.
Spreading love was his work.
Many sought to destroy him,
But he paid them no heed.
His only concern
Was for those folks in need.

His reality was dif'rent
From yours and from mine.
He had a dif'rent perspective
On life and on time.
He knew what was real
On a universal plane.
He knew that all life
Was really the same,

He laid down His life,
Not with sadness but joy.
For He knew that His body
Was only a toy.
He did not get caught up
In this worldly flame;
For He knew the importance
Of the Eternal Game.

Now, He came here to guide us
And to show us the light.
Things are not as we see them.
Death has no real bite.
Love rules o'er all life.
Love overcomes all.
Love is all that is needed
To correct "the fall."

His Hand Holding Our Hand

With His hand holding our hands,
    We are walking the road with Jesus,
        Sisters
           And brothers
              On our way.

Guided by Our Father,
    Surrounded by His Love,
        And His Spirit
           Lighting up
              Our way.

I Can Love

When the weather's kind of stormy
    And the sun don't shine,
I don't have to let it
    Worry my mind.
I can look up past the clouds,
    See the sunshine above.
Dark clouds can't bother me
    As long as I can love.

When my life doesn't go
    The way that I think it should,
When I can't seem to find my way
    Out of the woods,
I have to remind myself
    To not resist.
Loving every lesson helps
    Clear away the mist.

I BELIEVE IN LOVE

I believe in the moon
And the old Milky Way.
I believe there are rainbows
After the rain goes away.
I believe there is a sun
That shines up above.
And in my deepest heart
I believe in LOVE.

Love is not an emotion.
Love is cosmic glue.
It is the power of all life.
It is in me and you.
It flows through all the flowers
And all the stars above.
Everything that exists
Is made up just of LOVE.

There's no need to try
To change the way things are.
There is a master builder
Who's much better than we are.
He's the one who planned the eagle.
He also planned the dove.
He knows what He's doing.
He creates with HIS LOVE

THE INNER SPARK OF LOVE

Deep inside each individual lives
A spark, waiting to become a flame.
This spark glows when the person gives
Indication of awareness of the game
That is played out on the board of life,
And taken so seriously by those who play.
We believe that this reality of strife
Is, in truth, the only way
For us to spend our precious allotted time.
We pay no heed to the inner spark
That could show us the pattern of the rhyme,
But will not compete with our chosen lark.

To fan that spark into a fire
We must look past what seems to be real,
And follow the thin silvery wire
Of awareness to the golden seal
Of God's divine plan of orderly, manifest Love.
In this concept the power of the universe resides.
Creation fits this Divine Plan,
Just as the glove fits the hand
For which it was specifically designed.
It is our task to follow this flow
Of order, not to attempt to guide it.
It will give us all we need to know.

When we can turn loose of what we think we know,
There is hope for us to be able to learn
The reality of how things really go.
Wisdom is not something which we must earn.
The difference between knowledge and wisdom is plain.
God provides both wisdom and knowledge, of course.
But knowledge is acquired from experiences gained,
While wisdom comes direct from the source.
Our "inner spark" is the direct experience of
The personal, internal representative
Of God's divine, orderly plan of Love,
The most wonderful gift that He could give.

It's You and Me

It's you and me, that's what I see.
There's no other way that it can be.
If I'm for you and you're for me,
Then we can live in harmony.

Now that's the message of our song.
If the world would sing it all day long
We soon would find that nothing is wrong.
And we are all right where we belong.

When we work only for our self
We put the whole world up on a shelf.
Truth and light are not in personal wealth
But in contact with life and the spiritual self.

To get the picture you have to let go
Of all you think, you think you know.
The outer boundary is inside the whole.
And to use your mind is to confuse your soul.

We are on this journey together, now.
We have our guide to show us how.
But we cannot to our egos bow.
Disharmony we can no longer allow.

Together we travel on our way.
Blending just like the rainbow rays.
We combine to light the day,
And speak the Word we heard God say.

LET GO AND LET GOD

I met this wise old gentleman
    On a walk one Sunday morn.
He looked to be almost ninety,
    Sittin' rockin' on his porch.
He was strummin' on his guitar
    And singin' this song.
I just had to listen a bit
    Before I wandered on.

"Let go, and *let* God
    Give you guidance for your life.
He lives within you.
    He can guide you through your strife."

He stopped strummin' and smiled at me.
    He said, "Son, I have something for you.
There's a lesson you need to learn in life.
    It's in this simple tune.
You think you can make your life be
    What you want it to be,
What you don't know, is that it won't work,
    'Cause you're blind. You just can't see!

"You have to let go, and let God
    Give you guidance for your life.
He lives within you.
    He can guide you through your strife.
This world's not the reality
    We need to tune into.
The reality of this life
    Comes from inside you.

"By trying to force your life
    To fit the models that you see,
You only restrict yourself,
    And limit what you can be.
Let go of those limiting goals.
    Let your vision go a far.
Seek the part of you that is God.
    Then you'll see who you really are!

"Just let go, and let God
    Give you guidance for your life.
He lives within you.
    He can guide you through your strife.
    He can guide you through your life."

HIS SPIRIT IS INSIDE ME

My God is always here to guide me.
     I never have to search for Him.
For His Spirit Is inside me,
     I have a connection deep within.
I don't hassle with illusions.
     His love is all that has ever been.

There is no place He cannot reach me,
     No place too high, no place too low.
He is always right here beside me,
     Beside me no matter where I go.
All I have to do is trust Him,
     For I know He loves me so.

Yes, His Spirit is inside me.
     It can guide me every day.
Yes, His Spirit is inside me.
     It can always show the way.
I don't ever have to worry.
     He always creates a sunny day.

Joy

Oh, what a joyful state is mine
If I just don't resist it.
This world is God's Design.
His Holy Love has blessed it.

I'm not here to criticize.
I'm here to enjoy it.
Everything is just my size,
Even though I might not know it.

God created this world for me.
He knew just what I needed.
But, I may not be able to see
The perfect pattern He heeded.

Not knowing just what needs to be
I have the book but can't read it.
I need to just follow His lead,
And tend the garden He seeded.

LOVE IS YOUR WAY

Father, You've told us
    Love is your way.
Your Love will guide us
    To a better day.
Sometimes it's cloudy.
    Sometimes I can't see.
But, I will hold on to
    What you have told me.

        Father, I'm thankful
           For all you have given,
        For the lessons of earth,
           For the knowledge of heaven.
        Through all of the drama
           Of one thing I'm certain;
        Your Love will see me
           Through the final curtain.

                Your Love is the power
                    That lights up the day,
                Keeps the stars in their heaven,
                    Formed the Milky Way.
                Your Love formed man
                    And it made the earth.
                Your Love will guide us
                    To our new birth.

LOOK, LISTEN, FEEL

Look only for the Good.
　　You would be happy
If you could
　　Look only for the Good.
You would find
　　Peace of mind
If you would
　　Look only for the Good.

Listen only for the Love.
　　It contains all
You have dreamed of.
　　Listen only for the Love.
It is deep
　　Down inside,
Not above.
　　Listen only for the Love.

Feel only the inner Peace.
　　It is always
Within your reach.
　　Feel only the inner Peace.
You will find
　　There's peace of mind
Enough for each.
　　Feel only the inner Peace.

Mistaken Identity

We are the drivers
   Our bodies are our cars.
It is our decision where we go
   And where we want to park.
Some of us drive Corvettes,
   Others a Volkswagen Bug,
Some drive a Mini Minor
   And others a Greyhound bus.
But if we define who we are
   By the vehicle we drive
We are missing the whole purpose.
   We're not really alive.

These bodies we are living in
   Are just a temporary scene.
They are not the whole of us
   By any means.
For each and every one of us
   The story is the same.
Our bodies only help us
   To stay in this life's game.
There is a whole universe
   Beyond this physical world.
We experience glimpses of this fact
   When we are open to His Holy Word.

THE LOVELIGHT OF GOD

There is a light in each being on earth,
A spark of the Light of God.
Ours is the joy of knowing that light
And sharing that knowledge with all.
Love and the Light of God are the same.
No difference will ever be found.
The LoveLight of God is the Universe.
It includes every being on earth.

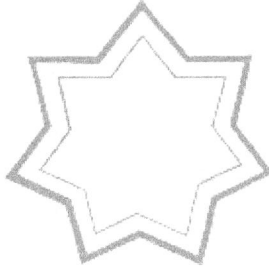

THE LOVE OF GOD

The Love of God will help you see
And open up the way.
It will show you how to be.
Show you a brand new day.

The Love of God is the cure
For all the ills you find.
It can make your pathway sure
And give you Peace of Mind.

THE LOVE OF GOD IS THE ORDER

Our Father is all knowing.
He has the plan.
Because of our limited perspective
We cannot see what He can.
Even when our lives seem troubled,
When we cannot understand,
He is the MASTER, THE ONE WHO KNOWS ALL.
Creating
As only
He can.

There is no need for us to see
The eventual end.
Because of our fears, our future He hides,
Those gifts brought by time's wind.
We walk our paths one step at a time
Guided by the Light He sends.
Our task is to follow the way that He leads.
Each step
A new journey
Begin.

Our fears will cease when we learn to trust
His Love to show the way.
His knowledge is ours whenever we ask,
Sure as night is replaced by day.
His Order of Love reigns supreme,
As even the stars will say.
OUR FATHER created a marvelous life.
His Power
Is ours
Always.

THE MASTER

One night as I walked in the moonlight,
  Down by the lake I did stroll.
There standing out on the water,
  There where no mortal could go,
That's where I saw The Master,
  On the water in the clear moonlight.
He gave me a gift that was priceless.
  He gave me a truth about life.

As I gazed at the man on the water
  I felt that I'd lost my mind.
No one can walk on water!
  That's as crazy as turning back time!
Then The Master said to come to Him.
  I told myself, " No, I can't go!"
He smiled and He laughingly told me,
  "Son, believing is what makes it so!"

Now, I never walked on the water.
  I think it was all a dream.
But sometimes I stop and I wonder.
  Some things just aren't what they seem.
When I run up against hardships,
  When I feel like there's no place to go,
I just think of the words of The Master,
  "Believing is what makes it so!"

MIRACLES OF LOVE

There was a time
I could not see.
The SPIRIT OF GOD opened my eyes.
A MIRACLE OF LOVE!

There was a time
I could not hear.
The SPIRIT OF GOD opened my ears.
A MIRACLE OF LOVE!

There was a time
I knew not love.
The SPIRIT OF GOD opened my heart.
A MIRACLE OF LOVE*!*

NOTHING NEED BE DONE

Our lives are filled with love.
Peace and light come from above.
Won't you share this love with me?
Peace, light and love are here.
We need to just let our sight clear,
Practice surrender and learn to just be.

Being is all that is needed.
If this guidance was just heeded
Then our night would turn to day.
We would not need darkness and night.
We would be able to see the light.
We would see love, joy and peace fill our way.

Nothing need be done!
We are all God's Holy Sons!
Perfection is all that can be!
I can only be what I am!
Share what I have, not take a stand!
I can love! I can flow! I can be!

Our Friend

When things don't go the way I want
    And life seems to frown on me,
When I get caught up in the fight
    For what I think should be,
When I find I'm pushing my point of view
    On those that are around me,
I just call upon my Friend
    And He helps me to see.

    He helps me remember that
        He is your Friend, too,
    We may have our differences
        In many things we do,
    But I don't need to change your ways
        Or your point of view!
    I can just know that our Friend
        Also takes care of you.

        If we'd just know that the Lord
            Leads each one on their way,
        Then people on the planet Earth
            Would find a brand new day.
        Though we might not always understand
            The many turns along the way,
        If each will simply do our part,
            His Peace will come to stay!

ONLY TRUTH REMAINS

I woke up this morning.
Saw another cloudy day.
I just started hummin'.
Blew those clouds
Away.

They weren't really clouds at all,
Just illusions of pain.
Painful clouds always disappear,
For only truth
Remains.

The things we see that we fear
Are never really there.
It's only misperceived reality
That makes our paths seem
Other than
Clear.

These illusions of clouds we see,
Our imagined strife,
Are not at all the way things are.
There's no need for
That part of life.

A clearer vision of our world
And God's great universe
Would help us see what clouds really are,
And know just what
They are worth.

*"And so they disappear to nothingness
Returning whence they came.
From dust to dust they come and go,
For only truth
Remains,"* *

* A COURSE IN MIRACLES Workbook p. 189, Foundation for Inner Peace, Tiburon, Ca. 1975.

Our Father's Song

We all have our dreams,
　　That fly on golden wings,
And form the melody
　　We sing along.
Little do we know
　　The melody that flows,
Is much more than just
　　Our simple song.

We each have our song,
　　The tune we sing along.
But all are pieces of our
　　Father's Plan.
A symphony He wrote
　　In solitary notes.
But each one to the others
　　Lends a hand.

As we each sing our songs
　　They combine and flow along.
We can begin to see the beauty
　　Of his plan.
Harmony is there.
　　There is no need for fear.
Our lives are just His Song
　　As played by man.

Our Love

My love I give to you.
  Nothing do I withhold from you
    For I am just
      Another you.

My life I've come to share with you
  To do the things we are here to do.
    For I am just
      Another you.

God has given us perfect love,
  Sunshine and rainbows and snow white doves
    God and you
      And I are love.

I am just another you.
  You are just another me.
    God and you
      And I are love

Pan's Advice

A wondrous sound
Quietly met me
   On a country road one day.
The source I found
Was a hole in the ground
   And a strange light lit up the way.
I followed the light
And found a beautiful sight
   For there way down in the ground
Sat fairies and elves
And unicorns, too,
   All listening to the sound.

And way up front
On a golden stage
   Sat Pan, their mythical god.
He sang about life.
He sang about love
   And the glorious paths that he'd trod.
I listened a while
To the joyous sound
   And I found I was getting mad!
These fairies and elves
Always enjoyed themselves.
   They seemed to never be sad.

Then I yelled good and loud.
I shocked the whole crowd.
   "This joy's only one part of life!
What about work?
What about worry?
   Or do only us humans have strife?"
Pan looked at me
With a steady gaze
   And said, "Son, you said it not I.
You humans create
Such a terrible mess
   By thinking you have to try."

You try to do this.
You try to do that.
 You try to do another thing.
You never go slow
Or watch for the flow
 Or go with just what life brings.
You use your mind,
Think your ideas are fine,
 Much better than all the rest.
But because you refuse
Your other gifts to use
 You miss out on all of the best.

Your life of pain,
Of clouds and of rain
 Is all that you'll ever know,
Unless you become
One of God's Loving Sons
 And join us in the flow.
God knows just
What He is doing.
 His Work doesn't need to be fixed.
Just learn to enjoy.
Find a way to employ
 All He has put into the mix.

The Pattern Master

The trail we walk can twist and turn,
    Sometimes up, and sometimes down.
But with every bend we learn
    A little more of what's around.

Our journey may seem hard
    With all the winding we must do.
But the route was made to fit our heart,
    Made to order for me and you.

There are no problems that we meet
    That are not there to teach
A better way to use our feet,
    And a quicker way our goal to reach.

And even though our brother souls
    May seem to block our chosen way.
They only point us to our goals
    Which are not always what we say.

Sometimes others serve us best
    When they force us to change course.
Or when they make us take a rest
    When we would some issue force.

The Master's view is not our own.
    He sees the whole, the all in all.
While we see only pieces alone
    And depend upon His guiding call.

But upon His vision we can rely
    And follow close the way He shows.
For He is Lord of earth and sky
    And knows just how the pattern goes.

PEACE DIVINE

Oh, what peace is mine,
   What joy, what bliss divine.
How sweet is the wine
   Of God's precious Love.

     It brings peace of mind,
       What a delightful find.
     You never need to unwind
       When you live God's Love.

Puzzle

While a few individuals may have glimpses of what is beyond the sensory realm, human experience of the universe is limited to what can be compared to a snap shot of nerve impulses received from the five sensory organs at any given moment. The mind strings these snapshots together to form thoughts. These thoughts are then strung together to produce a narrative or story that attempts to encompass the experience. The human mind can only process data "in context" or in relationship or comparison with other data, a narrative.

Narratives are neither right nor wrong, good nor bad. They are simply descriptions of sensory experience. A narrative that is tentatively accepted as a possible reality is a theory. Theories provide structure for focus but, by nature, structure imposes limitations on the data available for consideration, therefore limiting one's experience of reality.

A narrative that is experienced as reality itself becomes a belief. Belief limits any consideration or processing to only those data that are incorporated in the belief and so, severely constricts the individual's ability to experience anything other than the belief. Learning is a complete impossibility for those who believe they know, for they have nothing left open for consideration

Theories and beliefs are expressed in words that have
been accepted in cultural context as carrying "similar
internal   meaning" within the group. This is known
as a language. Languages are many and varied. They
are also neither good nor bad, right nor wrong. They are
simply more or less useful in particular situations with
particular individuals or groups.

Words are attempts of humans to communicate their
narratives or beliefs and theories. *Attempts* at communication
are the best we can hope for because there is no
way of determining if the words used in representing the
speaker's narrative are comparable to the narrative they
evoke in the listener.

Taking all of this into consideration, I have a problem. I'm
not sure whether I find it more amazing that humans can
take their beliefs based on such a limited perspective of a
limited sample of data and fight over who is right, or more
amazing that humans can actually think that they understand
each other.

THE REALITY OF LOVE

What is reality?
What do you see?
Is life on this level
What it seems to be?
What are the real questions
We need answers to?
Is there really something
We are here to do
BESIDES
LOVE?

Is there any purpose
Higher than His LOVE?
Is there any stronger light
Than the one from above?
How can we come closer
To the center of all things
Than to blend and merge
With everything life brings
AND
LOVE?

LOVE is the cosmic glue.
It binds me to you.
It is the sparkling dew
And lovely skies of blue.
It is the total pattern
That is formed by His hand,
The overall, complete
And comprehensive PLAN,
CALLED,
LOVE.

Recognition of Reality

My true will is
  Freely and knowingly
    Aligned with YOUR will.
In my deepest being
  I wish only to play my part
    In YOUR Divine Drama.

      My true thoughts
        Are but reflections
          Of YOUR thoughts.
      Through YOU
        My reasoning, understanding and attention
          Are clear and focused.

          My true heart
            Is filled
              With YOUR love.
          YOUR perfect love is
            Manifest through me as I participate
              In the unfolding of YOUR will.

Relationships

Our brothers and sisters are God's greatest gifts.
　　　They are our companions on our way.
Our task is not to judge them or to make them change
　　　But to love them, love them all, always.

Each one that we touch as we travel on our path
　　　Brings us Our Father's Gift of Love.
We can choose to accept this gift or pretend to let it lay,
　　　But it is ours, through them, from Him above.

Our brothers and sisters only bring us love.
　　　There is nothing else anyone has to give.
When they seem to bring us pain it is our mistake.
　　　We each choose the experiences we live.

If we just embrace all that comes our way,
　　　Accept the love in everyone we see,
With our brothers and our sisters we'll find joy and peace
　　　And realize how perfect everything can be.

Rightwork

It is the inalienable right of all sentient beings to make mistakes, experience pain, and even suffer if it is their wish.

It is their inalienable right to reduce their suffering by learning not to resist the inevitability of mistakes and pain.

It is their inalienable right to reduce their mistakes and pain by becoming increasingly aware of the laws of cause and effect and by increasing their awareness of, and surrender to, their greater understanding and knowledge of reality.

It is the true work of all sentient beings to foster these processes.

SOME THINGS ARE CERTAIN:

Night will yield to day.

What is truly ours

No one can take away.

Our wish to control

Causes the suffering we feel.

Following His lead

Will show us

What is real.

SHARING LOVE

This life seems so complex today.
    There are pushes and pulls from every way.
Some want it this way and other's don't.
    All some folks can say is, "I won't".
How can a body find stability
    In a world where so few are able to see
That what's important is that we care
    And that we, somehow, learn to share?

We look at each other and say,
    "I would do it a different way."
But we don't know how things really are.
    We're all following our own star.
I can't tell you which way to go,
    But I can help you reach your goal.
The help you need is not a shove,
    But for me to share my love.

I don't know what I'd do
    If I had to decide for you.
I can't say how I'd feel
    If I had to make your deals.
I might not see things just your way,
    I may not know the right words to say,
But there's one thing I know is true.
    I can share my love with you.

The Silence of Wisdom

I could never tell you
   What I want you to know.
      Just as my life is someplace
         You can never go.
Life is so very different
   For you and for me.
      But each one of us
         Is just what we need to be,

Words are for talking
   But who knows what they mean.
      Life can't be explained,
         Not by me, anyway.
There are no words that can tell
   The things I know are true.
      Knowing comes from living,
         Being what is you.

As much as I would like
   To share my love with you,
      Words will not allow
         The meaning to come through.
Living, loving, and knowing,
   Are not always understood.
      And I'm not sure we would want to,
         Even if we could.

SONLIGHT

The Son shines on the mountain top.
  He shines on the valley below.
The Son shining above the clouds
  Gives light when it rains where we go.
No matter where we may be
  The Son always shines, we know.
    He makes the whole world glow.

SonLight and life are one and the same.
  We find them where ever we go.
There is no beauty without the Son.
  Flowers in the wind could not blow.
He sends Heaven's light through misty dark clouds
  To light our way here below.
    He makes the whole world glow.

SonLight is beauty, is soft and is bright.
  His power controls the flow
Of energy around the earth,
  A delight to all who behold.
From the light He sends we begin to see,
  Our Father loves us so!
    He makes the whole world glow.

THE STORM

Sailing through the night
    A ship is making it's flight.
Fleeing the approaching storm,
    Inside all is safe and warm
        But the storm is moving on.

The wind whips through the sails.
    The ship begins to fail.
The mast snaps from the pressured pace,
    The ship can no longer race,
        But the storm is moving on.

The ship is petrified.
    All is cold and dark inside.
I'm all alone, surrounded by sea.
    What a frightful place to be.
        And the storm is moving on.

Then the ship is struck by a thought,
    I shall not come to naught.
I am just a small part of the sea,
    I am the storm and the storm is me,
        And we are moving on.

There Is Nothing To Fear

There is nothing to fear.
God's love rules here.
There is nothing to fear.
He holds each one dear.
There is nothing to fear.
If his voice is all we hear
There is truly,
Truly, nothing here
To fear.

THE STREAM

There once was a stream in a peaceful land
  With waters sparkling and pure.
He was a source of strength and calm.
  Most upsets he could cure.
He flowed between two peaceful towns
  In the valley where he lived.
Much enjoyment and pleasure were theirs
  From the waters he did give.

The beaver colony built a dam
  And lived within his midst.
Deer and birds could be seen
  Along his banks in the morning mist.
Then the people who lived in the towns
  Began to disagree over petty things
Like money and goods. More profits
  They wanted to see.

Their disharmony spread and broke the peace.
  Soon a war began.
The fighting there between the towns
  Disrupted the whole land.
The stream was used to calming things.
  He was feeling very low.
He asked the Father up above
  To give him more control.

"Father send me rains to fill me up
    And make me strong and great.
Then I'll sweep the valley and clean things up.
    I'll set those people straight!
With my rushing water I'll cleanse the earth.
    I'll wash their war away!"
The Father gently asked the stream,
    "Do you know the price you'll pay?"

"I don't care!" the stream replied,
    "They need to learn to love!
I'll wash away their petty hates
    With pure water from above!"
So the rains were sent and the river swelled.
    He felt his power rise.
He cleansed the valley and destroyed the war.
    He washed all beneath the sky.

The towns were flooded with his raging tide.
    The beaver dam was gone.
The children could not swim in him.
    He felt so all alone.
The birds and deer were not to be seen.
    Water covered the woods.
But most of all, to his dismay, his pure water
    Had turned to mud.

Surrender Is Peace

I surrender now.
    I surrender now.
        To Thy Will I humbly bow.
        I surrender now.
I open myself to You.
    I open myself to You.
        Serving Thy Will is all I can do.
        I open myself to You.
In my heart is Your Peace.
    In my heart is Your Peace.
        All of my struggles finally can cease.
        In my heart is Your Peace.

Surrendering

I don't know which way is up!
Nothing seems to be left in my cup!
There is nowhere I can see to jump!
My whole life seems to *be* over the hump.
With no direction that I can find
I don't know what to do with my time.
You'd think that I could do better than this.
It looks as if every shot was a miss.

The current pulls me on down the stream!
It's moving much faster, now, it seems!
I can't stop the rush of my pace!
I can only go along with the race!
There is no way that I can control
The direction or speed at which I go!
I can only surrender to that which IS!
And know that the decisions are HIS!

Sweet Perfection

The flowers show
  His beauty to me.
    The sky full of birds
      Tell me we are free.
There's nothing to do
  But be still and just be.
    Sweet perfection
      Is In all that I see.

    All nature sings
      In harmony.
        The universe flows
          Oh, so orderly.
    Nothing escapes
      His constancy.
        Sweet perfection
          Is In all that I see.

THAT IS LOVE

As I listen to the sound
Of the world goin' 'round,
There's only one thing
That sound can bring.
That is LOVE!

LOVE is the secret, the secret of birth,
LOVE flows freely all over the earth.
LOVE is the thing
That can make us sing.
That is LOVE!

There is nothing else in this life
That can overcome our illusions of strife.
There is only one way
To that clearer day.
That is LOVE!

LOVE is the essence, the essence of song.
LOVE heals all wounds and corrects all wrongs.
LOVE is the one
That can't be undone.
That is LOVE!

Thank You, Father

Father, you have given
    All that I need.
Nothing's left out.
    All could be received.
Nothing is lacking
    In Your universe.
You said, "It is GOOD."
    It's written in Your Verse.

Winds bring change,
    That's how it goes,
Just as the thorn
    Always grows with the rose.
Change always follows,
    As living proceeds.
Our task is to follow,
    Not to judge or lead.

Life's events
    Balance each other,
We free ourselves
    By loving our brother,
The suffering we see
    Is made by our minds.
Life really reflects
    Only Your Love, Divine.

Your winds of change
    Alter our lives.
We think we know
    What should survive.
We resist the thorns,
    And want only the rose,
But we don't understand
    How the Master's Plan goes.

So I thank you for
    The winds that blow.
I thank you, Lord,
    For the thorn and the rose.
Thank You, Father,
    For all the gifts that I see
And for the quiet assurance
    Your Love provides me.

THERE IS SADNESS

There is sadness. There is grief. There are things in this world that are not the way they should be. We think we know better. We think we know more. We think we can teach them how to live, how to learn to be free.

Yet, there still is sadness, anger and destruction. The world is a mess of war and hatred and not the way it should be! So we scold and blame them for not seeing the light, for following their own way, instead of learning to flow with what is and shall ever be.

We feel sadness. We feel grief. We feel the world should change to be the way we need it to be. What is the problem? What are we missing? Maybe we should practice the message we keep preaching and learn to just be.

Yes, there is sadness. Yes, there is grief. The world holds all things for us to see, to live, and to learn how to be. Nothing is wrong. There is no problem. We simply have not learned to accept what is and just be.

THE TRINITY

The Father is the Creative Force.
    He is the cause of all that ever exists.
His love holds together galaxies,
    And tiny specks of mist.
This energy of His is all that there is,
    And all that will ever be.
And He has told us all, many times and many ways,
    That we are heirs to all that we see.

The Father has many sons.
    They are spread both near and far.
We have an elder brother who watches over us.
    It makes no difference where we are.
He is here to help us and guide us,
    Our education He assists.
He helps us to see just what we can be,
    And our purpose here not to miss.

The Holy Spirit connects all God's sons
    From somewhere deep within.
He is the still small voice, the inner guide,
    Or just a feeling that's on the wind.
He's our instant connection with all that's right.
    He's with us each and every one.
With the voice of the Father and the strength of the Son,
    He blends us all into one.

WE ALONE

Just as the eagle flies alone,
  So every man must walk alone.
    Life is like that eagle's flight;
      Each must find his own light.
        We try and we try to find our own.
          No one else can show us home.
            We alone.

The eagle soars and flies on high,
  Hoping some morsel of food to spy,
    If he should fail he will surely die,
      Just as surely as you and I.
        We try and we try to find our own
          But no one here can show us home.
            We alone.

The eagle's alone but he is not lonely.
  He is the way he is meant to be.
    That is not true just for him only.
      It's just as true for you and for me
        We try and we try to find our own
          And we alone can show us home.
            We alone.

WHEN

When we learn to let our lives flow
      We soon find that love is all we know.
When we relax and just let ourselves be
      Then it seems that love is all we can see.
When we set our brothers free
      Then we will find our own freedom indeed.
When we can ourselves forgive
      Then love is all that we can live.
When we see that all life is one
      Then the Christ will surely have come.
When we are ready to see our destiny
      Then God can work through you and me.

Where Are The Answers?

Where are the answers? Which is the way?
  What am I to do with my life today?
Who will show me which way to go?
  Who will help me open the doors?

I'm so confused, so all alone,
  So isolated, so far from home.
I don't want to decide what I am to do.
  Will I make a bad decision if I try to choose?

No man is an island. So we are told.
  But in our decisions each stands alone.
No one can take from us the choices we make.
  They're ours alone, the joy and the ache.

Life is a puzzle. It's all a game.
  Do you follow your heart and make your own name?
Or do you follow the crowd and give them your power?
  Do you need to fit in or do you want your own hour?

Sometimes I wish I wasn't this way,
  Choosing my own path, going my way,
Deciding for myself which way to go.
  It was much easier when I was told.

Where are the answers? Which is the way?
  What am I to do with my life today?
No one can show me which way to go.
  I alone must open my doors.

YOU ARE THERE

I listen to Your rain that falls.
    I watch Your clouds float above.
I feel the coolness of Your breeze.
    I know the wonder of Your Love.
I smell Your flowers in the spring.
    I hear Your tiny song birds sing.
I see Your beauty everywhere.
    I know the peace Your Love brings.
I know the wonder of Love so great,
    The world is tiny by compare.
Your love enfolds me all around.
    Wherever I am, You are there.

YOUR LOVE

YOUR LOVE is on the hillside.
YOUR LOVE is in the sea.
YOUR LOVE is all around us.
YOUR LOVE is all that can be.
YOUR LOVE is in the baby.
YOUR LOVE is in the man.
YOUR LOVE is the flower
Of time since it began.

About the author:

Don Hickman lives with his wife Nancy in the woods overlooking the Mississinewa River south of Gas City, Indiana. They currently share their living space with an Akita dog, Kia, and a large yellow cat that helped raise her, Aries. The family also includes a large 20 yr. old Yellow Slider turtle named Grimace who will occasionally have a pet fish or two because she was not able to catch them for food.

Dr. Hickman began his educational career studying theology but soon discovered his calling in the field of mental health care. He has worked in this area since the mid '60s. Receiving his PhD in Clinical Psychology at the University of Arizona in 1977, he is licensed in the State of Indiana as a Registered Nurse and a Health Service Provider in Psychology. He continues his clinical practice in psychotherapy.